The Gift of Prayer

Written by GEORGE BICKERSTAFF

Illustrated by KEITH CHRISTENSEN

BOOKCRAFT INC.
SALT LAKE CITY, UTAH

Library of Congress Catalog Card Number: 74-33178
ISBN 0-88494-276-7

2nd Printing, 1976

LITHOGRAPHED IN U.S.A. BY
PUBLISHERS PRESS
SALT LAKE CITY, UTAH

"I'm glad school's out,
aren't you?"

"Yes, and we don't have
to go back until after
Christmas." Janet glanced back
at the school they had left a
few minutes ago.

"You know what I want for Christmas?" Susan didn't wait for Janet's answer but hurried on excitedly. "I want that lovely stroller that's in Riley's window, and the big doll by the side of it. And an oven, and a mixer with the cake mix stuff, and an iron, and…"

They were nearly home before Susan ran out of things on her list. Finally she asked what Janet wanted for Christmas. The reply came slowly and quietly.

"We'll be having a quiet Christmas, because my mommy is sick. All I really want is for her to be well again. I'm doing the dishes and the dusting and other things, so that she can rest more. And every day in my prayers I ask Heavenly Father to make her well soon."

"Dishes! I hate doing dishes!" Then Susan's frown changed to a grin as her next thought came. "I always leave them for Mommy to do. When there are dishes to be washed I do my piano practice, or some writing, or something else she won't want me to stop. Poor you, having to do dishes!"

"Oh, I don't mind," Janet explained. "Anyway, Daddy says that if we pray for something, we have to work to help Heavenly Father bring it about."

Susan was thoughtful as she walked up the steps of her home. If Janet could pray for something special, so could she. For those things she wanted for Christmas, perhaps.

She would try it this very night.

And she did. After she had said her usual prayer and her mother had tucked her in, Susan slipped out of the covers and kneeled by her bed. There wasn't much time, and she didn't want her parents to hear.

"Heavenly Father," she began, "for Christmas please may I have that nice stroller, and the big doll to go with it; and the mixer and the oven and the cake mix; and that cute iron and ironing board; and the other doll with lots of clothes to dress her up in." She mentioned several other things she would like. Then she closed her prayer, jumped into bed, and quickly fell asleep.

In the house next door, at about the same time, Janet too was praying. Her daddy knelt with her, their hands clasped together.

"Heavenly Father," she said, "I thank thee for all my blessings—for our nice home, our food and clothing, our health; and especially for the gospel we have, and for my mommy and daddy."

Daddy squeezed her hand as she went on. "My mommy is sick. Please bless her and make her well soon. I know thou canst do this. I love thee and want to do thy will. Please help me to. In the name of Jesus Christ, amen."

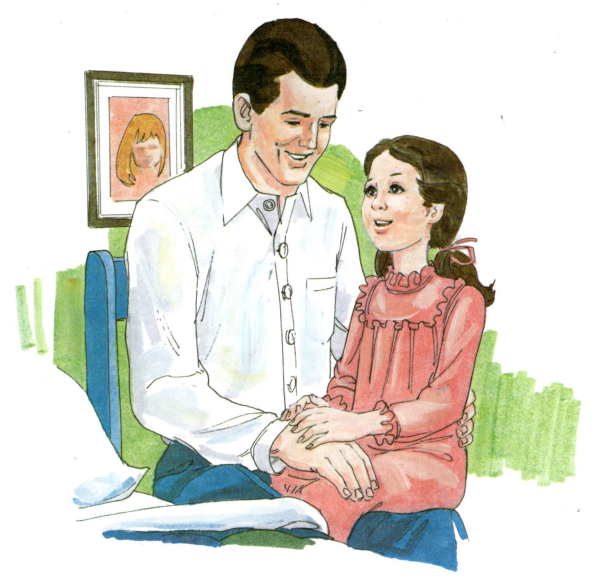

When Janet had finished, Daddy sat on the bedside chair and drew her onto his knee. "You know, Janet," he said, "I'm so proud of you. You are really learning how to pray."

"Did I remember everything, Daddy?"

"Pretty well. You were still and reverent. You called Heavenly Father by name; you thanked him for what you have; you asked for what you need; and you closed in the name of Jesus Christ. You remembered to use the language of prayer, too—thee, thou, and thy, and so on. Heavenly Father is so special to us that we don't use the everyday *you* and *your* when we speak to him. Right?"

"Right, Daddy. What else did I remember?"

"You remembered to tell him you love him. He likes to hear that, just as earthly parents do." And Daddy gave Janet a big hug.

While her arms were around Daddy's neck, Janet just couldn't help whispering in his ear, "I love you, Daddy."

Just then Mother called from the living room, where she was resting on the couch. "What are you two talking about? Come and share it with me."

Janet sat on the edge of the sofa holding her mother's hand while Daddy pulled up a chair to sit on. "We were talking about prayer," he said. "Janet asked Heavenly Father to make you well. And I feel sure he will, don't you, Janet?"

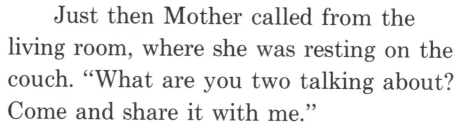

"Of course," was the reply. "Heavenly Father always answers my prayers—like the time I asked him to help me when I was to give a talk in Junior Sunday School, and he did."

"That's because you had prepared well and felt sure he would help you—that is, you had faith. When Jesus appeared to the Nephites he had some special things to say about prayer. He said that whatever we ask the Father for in the name of Jesus Christ, he will give it to us if it is right for us and if we have faith that we will receive it."

"How can we tell if it's right for us, Daddy?" Janet asked.

"Well, that can be a little tricky. It's true that we can't always tell for sure, but in any case we have to trust Heavenly Father to know best and to give us what is good for us—and that too is part of having faith in him. But if our prayer is unselfish, that's a good start. And yours was unselfish."

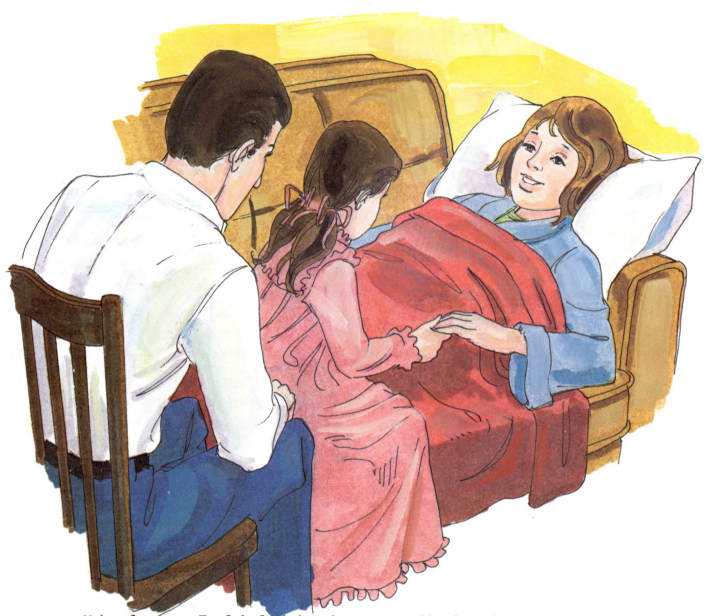

"And now I think it's time our little girl went to bed," said Mother.

"Let's have our evening prayer together, then," said Daddy, "and then we'll tuck her in."

"I remember that Jesus said something about family prayer, too," said Mother. "'Pray in your families unto the Father, always in my name, that your wives and your children may be blessed.' In family prayer, of course, one person prays for everyone there, and the rest think of what he is saying and then say 'Amen.' This makes it everyone's prayer. It's that way too with prayers in church."

Daddy helped Mother up, and they all went into the bedroom. While Janet knelt at the corner of the bed, her parents knelt one each side of her at the foot and side of the bed, and the three linked their hands.

After the prayer Janet stood up and put her arms around Mother and Daddy. "I'm so glad you taught me to pray," she said. "It's so special."

"It really is, sweetheart," said Daddy, "a very special gift from Heavenly Father. If it weren't for prayer, we would have no way to talk to him."

Janet was busy at home helping to prepare for Christmas, so she did not see Susan for several days. But the day after Christmas, Susan brought her new toys over for Janet to see.

"Oh, Susan!" Janet exclaimed. "What a beautiful doll! And that lovely stroller. And the iron and the mixer— why, you got everything you wanted, didn't you?"

"No, I didn't," Susan quickly replied. "I didn't get the ironing board or the oven, so I can't iron properly or make a cake. And I didn't get any extra clothes to go with the smaller doll. And after I'd asked Heavenly Father for them too. Still, I really didn't think it would be any good praying about it."

She glanced around the room. "Anyway, what did you get? Did you pray for Christmas presents?"

"I got this nice doll, and one or two other things," Janet replied. "We couldn't have an expensive Christmas, because Daddy has had so many doctor's bills to pay. But I got what I prayed for. Mommy is much better. She stayed up nearly all Christmas Day, and she's getting stronger all the time."

She turned to watch her mother go into the kitchen. "This is the best Christmas present I've ever had. Soon Mommy will be all well again."

Janet's eyes were glistening when she turned back to her friend. "Oh, Susan! I think it's wonderful how Heavenly Father answers prayers."

How Should You Pray?

1. Be still and reverent.
2. Call on Heavenly Father by name.
3. First thank him for your blessings; then ask for what you desire.
4. Always close the prayer in the name of Jesus Christ, and say "Amen."
5. Use the language of prayer.
6. Tell Heavenly Father you love him.
7. Ask him to help you keep his commandments. (Obedience shows you love him.)
8. Be unselfish in what you ask for.
9. Ask only for what you feel is right.
10. Feel sure you will receive the blessing you seek, if it is Heavenly Father's will. Don't doubt.
11. Do everything you can to help Heavenly Father answer your prayer. (These "works" go with faith.)
12. Pray often—always at morning and night, and whenever else you feel the need.
13. Pray both on your own and with your family.
14. In family or church prayers, follow in your mind the words being said. (Don't let your mind wander.) Say "Amen" at the end.